To

From

You're WONDER-FULLY made

A Book Written by Me about Amazing You

DaySpring
LIVE YOUR FAITH

YOU ARE

SO
MUCH
fun

TO BE WITH!

I laugh so hard when
I remember the time

you mean so much to me!

If you could listen to my prayers, this is what you'd hear me praying for you...

I *love* TALKING WITH YOU, SO OBVIOUSLY WE SHOULD START OUR OWN

Talk Show!

This is what we can call it and who we should have as some of our first guests:

FEATURING

If I could fly a plane, this is what I'd write to you in the sky:

you are
LOVED
by SO
many people!

If I designed T-shirts for your fan club, this is what they would say:

MAKING MEMORIES WITH YOU IS SOMETHING

I love to do!

Here is one of my favorites:

I love celebrating YOU!!!...

If I threw you a surprise party, this is what it would be like

SURPRISE!

LOCATION:

MENU:

ENTERTAINMENT:

GUESTS:

GIFTS I WOULD GIVE YOU:

YOU MAKE ME

SMILE

SO BIG!

Here are just a few of the reasons
I think you make God smile too:

BEING WITH YOU

Warms my heart.

These are some things
I'd love to do with you
on a perfect winter day:

IF I COULD CREATE A *holiday* IN YOUR HONOR, IT WOULD BE CALLED:

_____

And this is how everyone
would celebrate you:

IF WE COULD GO

anywhere together

ON A
TANDEM BIKE RIDE,

I'd take you to...

GOD MADE YOU SO WONDERFULLY

One-of-a-kind!

These are just a few
of the things that
make you so special
and unique:

IF I COULD
GIVE YOU A
special
AWARD,
IT WOULD
BE CALLED:

And this is why you deserve it:

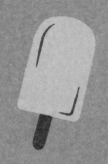

Plans with
YOU

are something
I love looking
forward to!

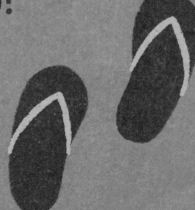

Let's plan a special day together next summer doing these summery things! (Can't wait!!!)

These are just a few of
the things I love about you:

YOU ARE AN ABSOLUTE

TREASURE

and I can't thank God enough for you!

you are such a gift in my life!

These are a few of the special ways you bless me just by being wonderful you!

I DON'T JUST THINK
YOU ARE AMAZING—

I KNOW
*You
are!*

If I had a megaphone to tell
everyone just how incredible you are,
this is what I would say:

If I
wrote a
Song
based on you
it would be called:

And these would be the lyrics:

Here are just a few ways your kindness shines through:

SO MANY THINGS REMIND ME OF

You!

You always come to mind when I read about this character in the Bible:

_____
_____
_____
_____
_____
_____
_____
_____

YOU BRING SO MUCH

joy

TO MY LIFE!

Here are just
a few ways you do it:

YOU HAVE AN

amazing

fan club

OF PEOPLE WHO LOVE YOU!

Here's what just a few of them had to say about you:

AMAZING

WAY TO GO

YOU ROCK

ADVENTURES
with you!

Here are just a few things
I hope we can do together soon:

YOU ARE SO
thoughtful
AND I AM SO
grateful
FOR THAT!

Here are just a few
of the ways you
show you care:

I BELIEVE IN YOU AND
YOUR DREAMS.

I'M PRAYING GOD
WILL BRING THEM TO
full bloom!

Here are a few of the things I am asking God to do in your life:

TRAVELING
WITH YOU

=

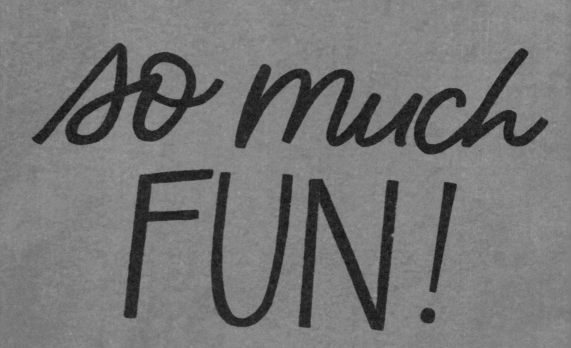

so much
FUN!

Let's plan a trip to_____.
This is what we would do there:

greetings from...

IF I THREW YOU A

Parade.

I'D MAKE A SPECIAL FLOAT
FOR YOU TO RIDE ON.

Spending time with you is the BEST!

LET'S PLAN A FUN DAY (just you and me) SOON!

Here's what we can do:

YOU AND I MAKE A
GREAT
team!

I think we would win if we
competed on this game show:

_____

This is what we would do
with our prize money:

GOD HAS A

HUGE
heart
FOR YOU.

In fact, I know He was smiling when He saw you...

Thank you for all the times you were there for me, especially when:

You are a
BRIGHT
LIGHT
in my life.

I *love* IT

WHEN YOU SHARE ABOUT WHAT GOD IS DOING IN YOUR LIFE!

I especially loved watching Him come through for you when...

IF THEY
MADE A
MOVIE
ABOUT US,

THIS IS WHAT IT WOULD BE CALLED:

_____

THIS WOULD BE THE PLOTLINE:

_____

_____

_____

_____

_____

_____

_____

_____

I LOVE ALL YOUR *kind,* *Caring,* & COMPASSIONATE QUALITIES!

Let's plan a special day to
serve the community together.

Here are a few ideas of how we could do that:

hehe!

haha!

YOU HAVE
SUCH A GREAT
SENSE OF

humor!

HA!

My favorite funniest memory
of you was when:

HA!

haha!

hehe!

I LOVE THE
WAY YOU
Bless
PEOPLE AROUND YOU!

Let's plan to do
something special for

_____

This is what we can do:

SPENDING TIME WITH

You AND Jesus

IS ONE OF MY
favorite
THINGS TO DO!

Lets read a book together that will help
us grow in our faith and talk about it.

Here is a list of books we could read and why I think we'd enjoy them:

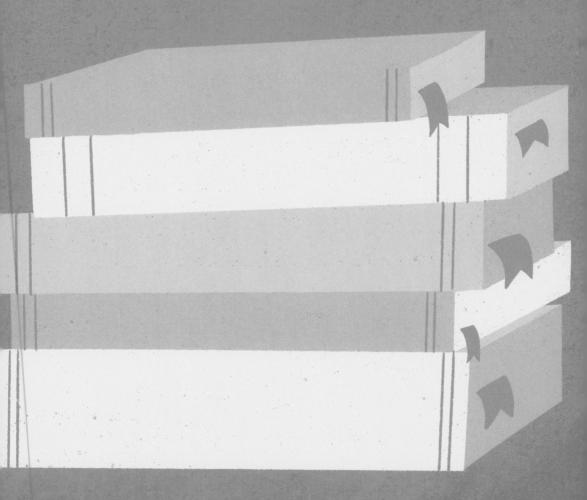

I love
talking
with GOD
about you!

This is what I'm asking Him to do in your life:

21154 Highway 16 East
Siloam Springs, AR 72761
Copyright © 2021 by DaySpring Cards, Inc.
All rights reserved.

Written by: Annie Scott
Cover Design & Illustrations by: Becca Barnett

Printed in China
Prime: J4965
ISBN: 978-1-64454-984-1